MALCOLM X

FOR BEGINNERS

BY BERNARD AQUINA DOCTOR

For Beginners LLC
62 East Starrs Plain Road
Danbury, CT 06810 USA
www.forbeginnersbooks.com

Text, Graphics and cover painting by Bernard Aquina Doctor and Aquina
Productions, NYC Copyright: © 1992 Bernard A. Doctor
Illustration Copyright: © 1992 Bernard A. Doctor
Cover Illustration Copyright: © 1992 Bernard A. Doctor
Cover Design Concept by Chris Hyde; Cover Design by Terrie Dunkelberger;
   type design & copy coordination by Josh Gosciak
Edited by Deborah Dyson
With special thanks to Glenn Thompson

A For Beginners® Documentary Comic Book
Originally published by Writers and Readers, Inc.
Copyright © 1992

Cataloging-in-publication information is available from the Library of Congress.

CIP 92-050419

ISBN-10 # 1-934389-04-8 Trade
ISBN-13 # 978-1-934389-04-1 Trade

Manufactured in the United States of America

For Beginners® and Beginners Documentary Comic Books® are published
by For Beginners LLC.

Reprint Edition

Contents

A Message from the Artist / Writer:

I was a child when Malcolm X was killed on February 21, 1965. I remember how cold it was in Harlem that year and the sense of anger, loss and frustration coming from most of the grownups when the news spread throughout the community: Malcolm X was shot; Malcolm X is dead. The mid-Sixties were a period of experimentation, hippies, drugs, free love, the peace movement, protest against the war in Vietnam. It was a turning point in America that put to test the principles of the entire nation.

Today, when it seems that most of the gains in the areas of civil rights are being rolled back one by one, it is more important than ever to rediscover the impact of leaders like Malcolm on our society. Since Malcolm's death, the Seventies and Eighties have brought frustration and apathy to replace the righteous anger Malcolm used to inspire an entire generation to act out for change. Malcolm was a remarkable human being and, in learning about him and what he stood for, it is important to learn about the total man, a complex individual who lived through many phases of recurring tragedy and emotional upsets which forced him to re-evaluate and restructure his life. Malcolm was strong, proud and eloquent and stood tall and, even in the last minutes of his life, he remained steadfast and dedicated to the struggle and philosophy of Black Nationalism. He understood he might one day be called to make the ultimate sacrifice for his beliefs, for his love of his people and for his God, Allah.

To me Malcolm was a prophet, a poet, a teacher and a true

Renaissance thinker. I had many gifted professors and instruc-
tors in art school and college and many of them played key
roles in my thinking and development, but Malcolm X, El Hajj
Malik El-Shabazz, was my Grand master. He taught me to face
up to and take total responsibility for my life, my achievements
as well as my failures, to be resolute in my thinking and to
stand up for what is right.

I believe this is Malcolm's message to us all. This book is my
token payback to a master of survival and the baddest brother
of recent history, Brother Malcolm X.

The realization of this book was made possible with the
help and encouragement of many friends and loved ones who
gave me counsul and support; Glenn Thompson, our visionary
leader, who first approached me with the project and gave me
total creative freedom; Deborah for her support and friendship
and for reminding me I really was getting it done when I couldn't
see it; Barbara for her time and advice and generosity; Larry
for the valuable tip; to the many in and around town who helped
me gather research and materials; to my soulmate Ro for
being there no matter what; to my best Buddy and confidente
Benny.

To my sisters, Rhonda and Yvonne, whom I love and shared
a third of my life with, and my mother, Lucille, for being my
mother, and Imani, this is my welcome-to-life gift to you.

To my furry assistants who kept me company during the
many all-nighters; Muffin and Yin Yin and beloved Coco Foo and
Nynja.

Peace, and power to the children.

Bernard Aquina Doctor
New York, NY 1992

Bernard Aquina Doctor is a writer and artist living in New York City. He received his art training at the High School of Music and Art and the School of Visual Arts, both located in New York City. A professional visual artist for more than 14 years, Doctor is a member of the Graphic Artists Guild of America. This is his first book.

Months before he was born, the home of Malcolm's parents was visited in the night by the Ku Klux Klan. The hooded night-riders were looking for his father. They left a message which turned out to be an omen of things to come for the unborn Malcolm Little. The message was, "stop spreading radical ideas about freedom, independence and equality among the negroes." They were going to lynch him in front of his family if he didn't. This was the beginning of a pattern of events that would plague Malcolm throughout his life.

Malcolm "X" was born May 19th, 1925, in Omaha, Nebraska. He was the fourth child of Earl and Louise and the seventh child of his father, who was also a seventh child. No surprise Malcolm adopted 7 as his lucky number.

Because of his mixed blood Malcolm was very unusual looking. His grandfather on his mother's side was Scottish, which gave Malcolm his light-skin and sandy-blond hair and eyes that were an unusual mixture of brown, blue and green depending on the lighting conditions.

Malcolm's mother always told him to "go out in the sun and get some color."

As a child Malcolm displayed exceptional intelligence, spending many hours browsing through his picture books. Malcolm learned early in life that by speaking out and making a fuss he could usually get what he wanted. His brothers, Philbert and Reginald, were his constant companions and even though they fought like cats and dogs always joined forces to look out for one another.

Malcolm's father was a poor country preacher and Malcolm recalls how his parents were always arguing and there was never enough to eat. Malcolm was close to his father and often went along in his father's old touring car to Garveyite meetings, where Malcolm received his first lessons in self-pride.

Marcus Garvey was a charismatic leader with a plan to unify the negro community. He dressed in elaborate uniforms trimmed in gold and wore a field marshall's hat reminiscent of Napoleon.

Marcus Garvey founded the United Negro Improvement Association to build a society economically independent of white America, with property, industries, services and trade. He wanted to establish trade agreements with other countries, particularly Africa and the Caribbean Islands. He outfitted an all-Black militia to parade through the streets of Harlem and other cities in the United States.

Marcus believed women had a prominent role in the U.N.I.A. and organized the BLACK CROSS to rival the White Cross philanthropic league; women also marched in the Black Militia.

Marcus established the BLACK STAR Steamship line,
a fleet of giant freighters to transport cargo and,
eventually, the Black community to African soil where
a new nation could be founded. Garvey wanted to run
all European whites out of Africa,

by force if necessary.

To support his grand schemes, Garvey raised millions from Afro-Americans. To stop Garvey, the U.S. government invoked a federal regulation which prohibited use of the mail to raise funds for any enterprise that could be viewed as a threat to national security.

Marcus Garvey was imprisoned in a federal penitentiary in Atlanta, Georgia, and after serving five years of his sentence was pardoned by President Calvin Coolidge in 1927 and deported.

Severed from his power base in the States, Garvey returned to Jamaica where he faded into obscurity. In the years that followed, his multi-faceted enterprises collapsed. Garvey is remembered for his slogan, BLACK IS BEAUTIFUL.

To escape the oppressive racism in Omaha, Malcolm's family moved to East Lansing, Michigan, but they found the same overt racism and bigotry there also. In Lansing, the Ku Klux Klan regularly marched through the streets and negroes were subjected to curfews that prohibited them from being out after sundown.

Earl bought a farmhouse outside of town and he continued to preach and organize for Marcus Garvey until a local hate group focused on him and threatened him.

Then, the realtor who sold the house to Louise, thinking she was white, later uncovered a clause in the deed that prohibited negroes from buying the property. They did not return the money and wanted Earl and his family to move out immediately.

The week they were to be evicted, the house was mysteriously set on fire in the early morning. Malcolm, his brothers and sisters and his mother and father were all forced out into the night and the firefighting squad let the house burn to the ground. These were chaotic, unhappy days for the entire family and Malcolm was deeply affected by it all and couldn't understand why it was happening.

A year later when Malcolm was six his parents had another terrible fight. Malcolm remembered the fight had something to do with a rabbit Earl wanted Louise to cook. When she refused, he killed it and threw it at her and stormed out of the house.

Earlier that day Louise had a premonition that something terrible would happen to Earl if he went out that night. The next day he was found by the railroad tracks barely alive. His skull was smashed and his body crushed and nearly cut in half.

It was suspected Earl was killed
by a white racist gang.

He stayed alive in that condition long enough
to tell Louise that the family would be all
right after the two insurance policies
he had taken out paid off.

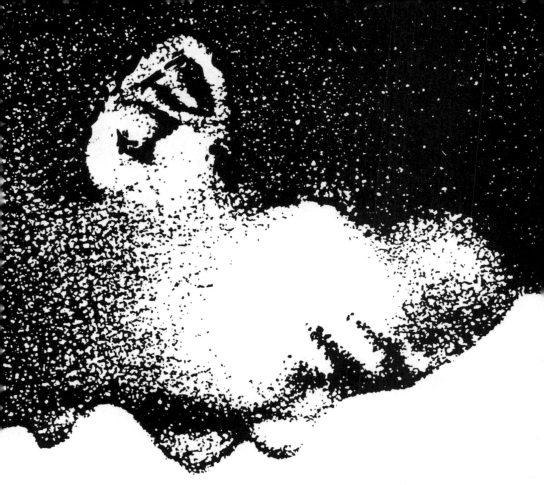

However, one of the companies refused to pay. They called Earl's death suspicious and had it classified a "suicide."

After Earl died the family had no income and there was never enough to eat. Malcolm became harder to manage and like any average boy was always getting into trouble. He took to stealing fruit and cookies from the local general store to supplement his diet.

Malcolm went rabbit hunting
with the adults and learned

to set
traps for
the rabbits
where they
would run
into, after
being
chased by
the dogs.

He also learned there was a system to catching fish and caught more than anyone else.

Later in life Malcolm reflected on these lessons and said, To survive, the negro has learned to adapt and knows more about the white man than the white man knows about the negro.

As Malcolm grew older he became aware of the stigma that his father's reputation and death had on his family. It was common knowledge in

town that the insurance company had cheated them and caused great hardship on the family.

Malcolm's mother, Louise, was a pretty woman with fair skin and straight black hair and, unlike Earl, she had received an education which was the cause of many fights between them. She often resorted to passing as white to get work. Malcolm recalled that she was fired on the spot when one bigoted employer discovered she was Black. For a long time she managed to provide meals from day-old bread and wild vegetables from the field until finally she applied for welfare assistance. Welfare workers were constantly visiting and separating the children to ask them probing questions, such as why was Malcolm so much lighter than the other children, and which one was smarter.

Malcolm felt these
intrusions were meant
to disrupt the family and set them against one
another. Eventually Louise suffered a mental
breakdown, became depressed and lost all inter-
est in everything. Malcolm felt the state helped
push her to the breaking point with their probing into the family's affairs.

Around the time Malcolm was placed with a foster family, Louise was placed in a mental institution. With no mother or father to guide or love him, Malcolm somehow managed to stay out of trouble. He improved so much in school that he was elected class president. He went out for the basketball and soccer teams and tried boxing but gave it up after losing his only two matches to the same opponent.

Malcolm was intro-duced to stereotyp-ing as the only prominent Black male in his school.

He was made the target of cruel pranks and set up to play out a role as a sexual stud.

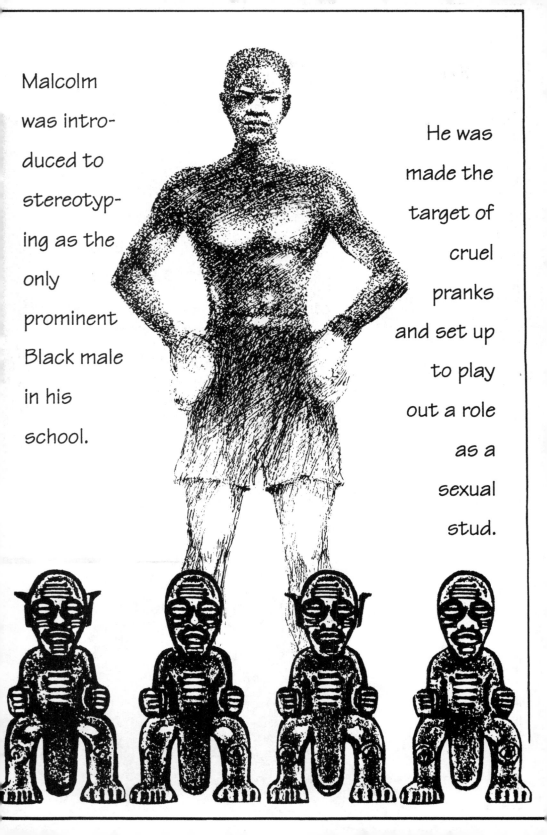

The constant racial slurs from the teachers, classmates, and his guardians began to get to him.

His teacher advised him against becoming a lawyer, instead he encouraged him to do something with his hands, like carpentry. Other students in his class were told to do whatever they wanted in life even though their grades were not nearly as good as Malcolm's.

Without access to a broad-based education and history, Blacks had little reason to believe they had a heritage other than what was taught in the schools and the school's library had very little on the history of African Americans except references to slavery, ministrel dancers and natives living in the jungles of Africa.

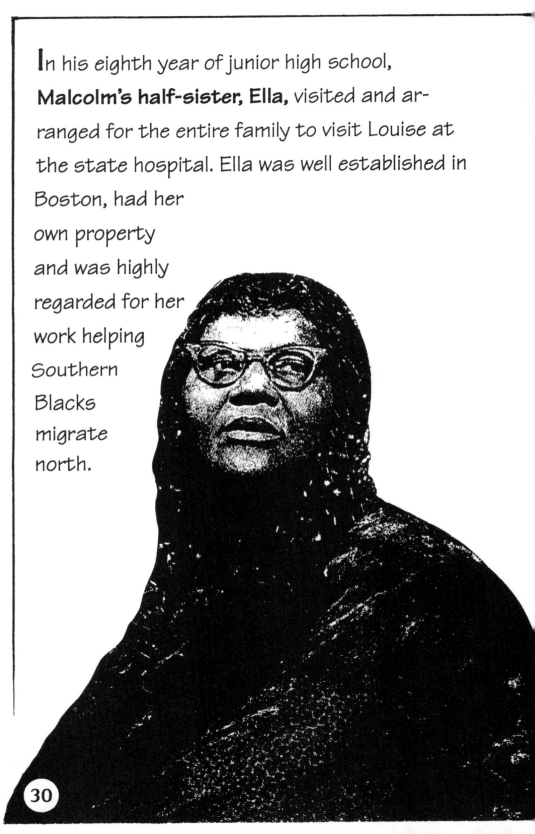

In his eighth year of junior high school, **Malcolm's half-sister, Ella,** visited and arranged for the entire family to visit Louise at the state hospital. Ella was well established in Boston, had her own property and was highly regarded for her work helping Southern Blacks migrate north.

This was Malcolm's first visit to Boston and he was so impressed by its energy he decided to live there. In the meantime Ella managed to obtain custody.

First Malcolm toured the city, marveling at the many historical memorials to American heroes, many of whom were Afro-Americans, such as Crispus Attucks, Frederick Douglass and . . .

. . . the fighting 54th regiment

of Black freed slaves, whose bravery in the battle of Fort Wagner opened the door for many
thousands more to fight and help win the war
against the South.

Malcolm felt rejected by the bourgeois Blacks Ella wanted him to associate with. He saw them as working class though they acted as though they were upper class.

Ella was disappointed when Malcolm gave up school and began hanging out on the streets. At a pool hall Malcolm met "Shorty" who was also from Lansing and who took an immediate liking to Malcolm. Shorty schooled him on how to dress and be "hep" and "cool." Shorty helped him "conk" his hair and buy clothes on credit to match his new look.

37

Dressed in his flashy zoot suit with hanging gold chain and pointy-toed shoes, Malcolm Little had transformed himself into "Detroit Red." He began to associate with a wild crowd, drinking, smoking and gambling.

He worked as a valet in the men's room of the Roseland State Ballroom, where he hustled his customers for tips. He sold or acquired for them anything from shoe strings to liquor and drugs.

When he was off duty he would go to the dances and watch the shows. He learned all the latest dances, made friends of the musicians and generally had a good time. After conquering his shyness around women, Malcolm grew so popular he soon had a series of girlfriends. He began seeing a Black girl who lived in the neighborhood where he worked as a soda jerk in a drug store. Ella was happy he had found a nice girl to spend his time with.

Malcolm met Bea at the Roseland, who later became his favorite girlfriend. Ella was shocked when she met Bea and refused to put up with his carrying on any longer. Bea was white.

While he lived in Boston, Malcolm had a series of jobs. The job that would eventually take him to New York was a job as a fourth cook on the railroad.

At the Roseland he had been entertained by the stories of how cool Harlem was and he knew he would end up in New York.
Malcolm learned that by acting like a clown to entertain the passengers he could get big tips. At times he went too far and some of them complained.

By the time he arrived in New York he was fired, but by then it didn't matter. New York was the largest city he had ever been in and there was so much more to do and get into.

Malcolm toured the city just as he had Boston. He soon discovered the "in" places like Small's Paradise, the Savoy Ballroom and the Apollo Theater. He rented a room in the Braddock Hotel on 126 Street behind the Apollo Theater and soon was on a first name basis with hustlers, thieves, prostitutes, pimps, addicts and dealers.

Malcolm lived by his wits from day to day, constantly watching his back and sinking deeper into the underworld.

At the height of World War II the government caught up with Malcolm and called him downtown to register for the draft.

Malcolm felt the army offered nothing but humiliation and servitude to white soldiers. Besides it was "uncool" for a "hep cat" hustler to be caught in uniform; it was bad for the image.

He went to the recruitment office acting like a crazed Black militant and convinced the army psychologist that he wanted to "get into uniform, get a gun and go South and organize Blacks to 'shoot up whitey.'"

For all his acting, Malcolm was still vulnerable. A loner, he was a small fish in an
ocean of bigger fish. He got ripped off by
other hustlers and was under constant
surveillance
by the
police.

49

Desperate, he teamed up with a pimp called "Sammy" and they became armed thieves until things fell apart after a few close calls when they were nearly caught by police.

Malcolm went from one hustle to another, but he had made some dangerous enemies and the police were still looking to bust him.

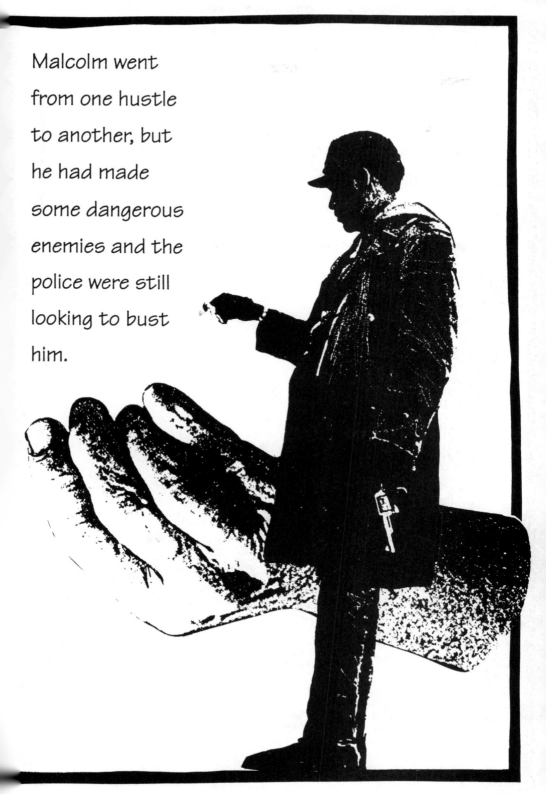

Finally, a showdown with a Harlem policy rack-eteer named "West Indian Archie" convinced Malcolm it was time to leave Harlem. He returned to Boston where he organized a gang which included his girlfriend Bea, her younger sister and Shorty. They burglarized apart-ments and pulled rip-off scams.

In January 1946 he returned to a jewelry store to pick up a stolen watch he had dropped off earlier for repairs.

The proprietor matched the watch against a list of stolen property and notified the police. They were waiting for him and took him into custody without a fight. This was the end of his life of crime and the beginning of a new phase in his life that would also be marked by racial injustice and double standards.

Malcolm and Shorty were sentenced to ten **years** and Bea and her sister were given one year on probation. He knew that as a first offender his sentence should not have been so harsh. This was a clear message that he was being punished for associating with two white women.

lcolm was 21 years old when ...as sentenced to ten years at Charlestown Prison. Charlestown was a medieval facility with no running water. The bathroom in each cell was a bucket and a basin filled with stagnant water. The cells were tiny and dirty and rodents and vermin were everywhere, even in the food and drinking water. Malcolm was crowded with other convicts in cramped quarters and had to contend with vicious, abusive guards. He felt like an animal in a pen.

He grew bitter and angry, lashed out at the guards and other prisoners, refused to cooperate and was put into solitary confinement. The other prisoners nicknamed him "Satan" because of his anti-religious outbursts.

Most thought he was insane and stayed clear
of him. Then visits from his brothers and
sisters began to bring him around.

They told him that it was no accident he was given so long a sentence and that he and so many other Black men had ended up in prison. They told him about **the Honorable Elijah Muhammad** and how the **Nation of Islam** was a new religion for Black people only that would explain everything and show him how to turn his life around.

T

he NOI taught that Black men were direct descendants of a race which lived thousands of years
ago called Original man. They were highly evolved, knew
the secrets of na-
ture and were in
communication
with giants on
Mars. An evil Black
scientist named
Yacud created
the white
race from
genetic ex-
peri-
ments.

This race of "devils" was corrupt but very intelligent. It was prophesied that they would rule the world with war, greed and hatred and create chaos and hell on earth for Black people.

62

After the white race destroys itself, the descendants of Original Man would inherit the earth and bring back peace and tranquility.

Malcolm reflected on his life and thought the Honorable Elijah Muhammad seemed to have the answers he was looking for. After he lost both parents his life lacked discipline and direction.

The Nation of Islam and Elijah Muhammad was a strict organization which
offered him a life of self-control.

Malcolm found new purpose in his life. He
knew he would never go back to his
former life or behavior.

He saw an opportunity
to rebuild himself and began to re-educate him-
self. He wanted to write
to his new mentor
but discovered his
reading and writing
skills were
so poor he
was barely
literate.

He vowed to re-educate himself and improve his writing, vocabulary and penmanship. He opened the dictionary to the first page and began to read and write down every word and its meaning and discovered a whole new world of knowledge and power.

Ella used her influence to get Malcolm transferred to an experimental prison called Norfolk. At Norfolk, Malcolm had a private room and unlimited access to a well-stocked library of books on every subject. He studied day and night even after lights out.

Malcolm said "Muslims don't believe in a heaven or hell after death. Black people are catching hell right here on earth in this life."

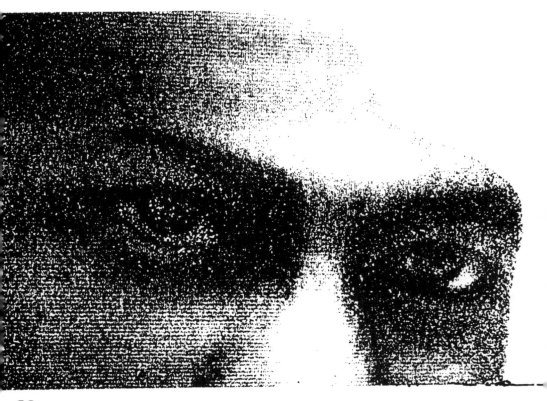

Malcolm was released from prison after seven years. He joined NOI and moved in with his brother Wilfred who was a minister of a temple in Detroit. He dedicated his life to being a Muslim and a student of Elijah Muhammad.

Malcolm worked in a factory until he found a better job in a furniture store. He felt he had a debt to repay to society for the person he once was and the things he had done. He was determined to make up for a wasted life.

While living with his brother's family he was touched by the love, respect and sense of togetherness shared by followers of the Nation of Islam. When he wasn't working, Malcolm assisted his brother at the temple in Detroit.

His hard work "fishing for converts to Islam" won him the favor of Elijah Muhammad and he was asked to speak about his life-experiences at meetings.

In the beginning, Malcolm spoke to small groups at these storefront temples, where he mostly repeated Elijah Muhammad's preachings, but soon developed his own style. He criticized the negro for wanting to please the white man in hopes he would be accepted.

"There are two kinds of negroes, the house negro and the field negro. One lives in the big house and takes better care of the white man than he does his own family. Then there is the field negro, who lives outside in the field and does everything he can to hurt the white master."

Negro leaders today are too busy fighting one another; it's become a matter of the "pot calling the kettle black." "We need to stop letting outsiders see us criticizing one another. It looks bad and it doesn't help solve our problems. We need to take it off the streets and keep it behind closed doors."

Malcolm was
so successful
at increasing
membership
that he was
sent to other
cities to start
new temples. He was promoted to the post of
assistant minister in Detroit.

Elijah Muhammad
was often ill
and could not travel,
so he sent Malcolm
or his other ministers
to represent him at meetings
and rallies. Malcolm
excelled as a speaker
and his personal appeal
made him a celebrity.
It was decided that
Malcolm be the new
minister of Temple No. 7
on the corner of Lenox
and 116 Street.

Malcolm was also named spokesman and chief representative of the NOI and heir-apparent to the leadership of the Black Muslim organization. Meetings in the temples were closed to whites. The press and cameras were also banished from these meetings. Malcolm felt whites would distort everything they heard at Black Muslim meetings.

*B*lack Muslim meetings were "for family only." The first priority of the community should be to pull together and seize our neighborhoods. Control our economy, our security and the education of our young.

Malcolm said that whites can help us by going back to their own communities and work to change their neighbors' attitudes toward Blacks.

Malcolm stressed Black pride and love of our heritage. "We have been so thoroughly conditioned as a people, we no longer even know who we are."

Soon membership in the Harlem temple grew to even greater numbers and Malcolm was rapidly building a following of his own. He always began his speeches by giving praise to Allah, then attributed his words as those of Elijah Muhammad.

He had a gift for sensing the mood of the crowds and keeping them involved. Many of his old street hustler buddies joined the NOI because of Malcolm.

The "Hinton Incident" brought national attention to the Black Muslims. In 1957 a street fight attracted several Muslims from Temple No. 7 who observed as the police arrested the suspects. When ordered to move on, they refused and Charles Hinton, a Black Muslim, was struck by a policeman.

Malcolm called the "Fruit
of Islam" guards to march
to the police precinct.
They stood silently while
Malcolm demanded to see
Mr. Hinton and insisted
that he be taken to the
hospital to receive medical
attention.

"It's a crime in the face of all the violence that's been perpetrated on the negro to expect them to be nonviolent."

> **"E**xpecting the white police to look out for us is like putting the fox in charge of guarding the chicken house.**"**

"The problem of the Black man in this country is beyond the ability of Uncle Sam to solve it. It's beyond the ability of the United States to solve. The government isn't capable of hearing our problems, much less solving it. It's not morally equipped to solve it."

One of the
officers who
witnessed
the formation
of silent Black
Muslims said,

"No one man
should have
so much
power."

From that day on there was always a full complement of riot police at his gatherings to "keep the peace." Some insiders in the NOI felt he was too ambitious and too activist. He ignored the writing on the wall that hinted he was rapidly reaching a point where he would have to start looking out for himself.

Racism is an ugly monster that is as alive in America today as it was in Malcolm's time, devouring the soul of the country.

In the Sixties, a mood of restlessness and impatience with the status quo brought a new president, John F. Kennedy, and vice president, Lyndon Johnson, into the White House. They promised wide-sweeping changes in the civil rights laws.

Malcolm was an eloquent and powerful debater. Many times his opponents never bothered to show up, knowing they couldn't compete against him. But being at odds with his mentor was the last thing Malcolm expected. It never entered his mind.

"Compared to the Honorable Messenger of Allah, I am nothing," Malcolm would say. Tired of being misquoted in the press, he designed and published a newsletter that would be the uncensored, un-edited voice of Elijah Muhammad called, Muhammad Speaks.

BLACK POWER

Malcolm was credited as the first to speak about Black self-defense and militancy, the philosophy of Black activism, and the need to take a stronger stand to gain control of our destiny. He was credited with the phrase, "BLACK POWER."

Later other voices would join him, some more militant than Malcolm, such as H. Rap Brown of the Student Non-Violent Coordinating Committee, SNCC, and the notorious Robert Williams who wanted to "BURN AMERICA TO THE GROUND."

Others included Stokely Carmichael, also from SNCC, and Eldridge Cleaver and Huey P. Newton from the Black Panther Party.

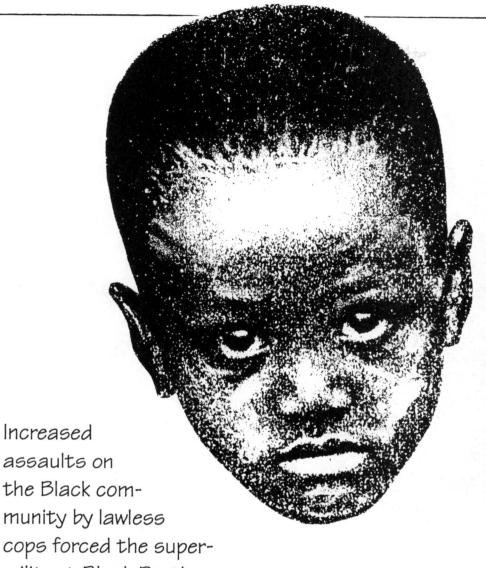

Increased
assaults on
the Black com-
munity by lawless
cops forced the super-
militant Black Panther
Party out on the streets, armed and prepared
to confront the "pigs" who patrolled the Black
community. The aim was to stop the killing and
brutalizing of Black men and women at the
hands of the police and other racist groups.

Malcolm said, "If we don't protect ourselves no one else will, certainly not the police."

Martin Luther King, Jr. was in direct opposition to Malcolm's methods and philosophy. Dr. King preferred to teach nonviolence and peaceful protest to effect change.
"Turn the other cheek and love thy enemy."

COMMEMORATE THE MURDER OF DANIEL BELL MARCH FOR JUS...

...eral hundred people gather for a 'M...h fo... stice
...leaders are saying they want th...
...st A Goddamn Nigger Kid'

...enty-One Years Later,
...hite Cop Admits Killing
...ack Milwaukee Man

Text and Photos by
D. Michael Cheers

...e day after Daniel Bell's 22...
...birthday he was shot and ki...
...a White Milwaukee polic...

Dr. King was awarded the Nobel Peace Prize for his work as an advocate of peaceful civil disobedience. But before he was assassinated in 1968, Dr. King was forced to reconsider his views.

Like his followers, he was beaten by police, thrown in jail, and denied his civil rights. Malcolm said, "give me a .45 caliber, then I'll sing 'We Shall Overcome.'"

MUSLIMS PRESS FOR RACE SEPARATION

Pending civil rights legislation required the full and total integration of all citizens in the areas of, as well as including access to, education, voter registration, employment, health care and housing. Philosophically, Malcolm agreed with the Black Muslims on the issue of integration. They wanted no part of it. They believed America was a doomed society.

The Black Muslims wanted a separate Black community. They reminded America of the promise made to the slaves after the emancipation proclamation:

"FORTY ACRES AND A MULE."

"The negro has taken care of the white man for over four hundred years. Now that the negro wants to look out for himself he is called racist and separatist."

109

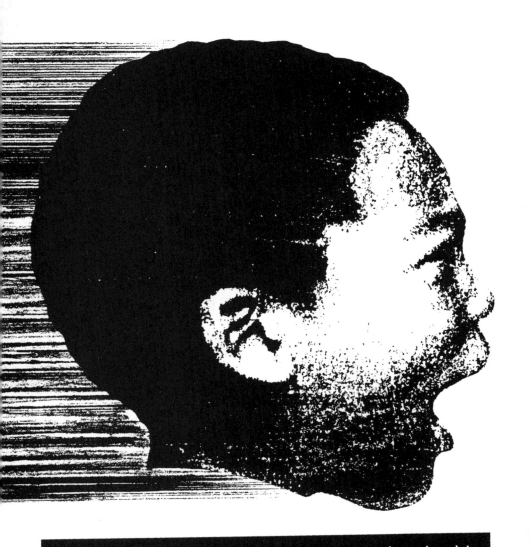

As late as 1964, Blacks were being lynched in America. Yet many Americans denied there was a racial problem at all.

WHITE POWER

A reporter asked Malcolm the question, "Does the Black man hate the white man?" Malcolm grinned and responded. "That's like asking the victim of rape if she hates the person who raped her, or a wolf asking the sheep if it hates him. The white man is in no moral position to accuse anyone else of hate."

In 1943, a fourteen-year-old boy was burned at the stake in Malcolm's home town of Omaha, Nebraska. The men who did it proud-ly posed for a picture of the ghastly crime while the body smouldered.

ONLY

THE REAL

POWER

in this society comes
from either the ballot or the bullet.

After President Kennedy was assassinated in late 1963, Malcolm was under strict orders not to make any comments to the press, but in confidence he made a brief comment to a reporter. He was stunned when he heard the evening broadcast.

MALCOLM X SAYS
"THE PRESIDENT
GOT EXACTLY
WHAT HE
DESERVED."

Malcolm meant to say "What had happened was the result of a climate of hate. It's a case of the chickens coming home to roost."

Malcolm understood that many Americans feared the President's policies would put Blacks on an equal level with whites.

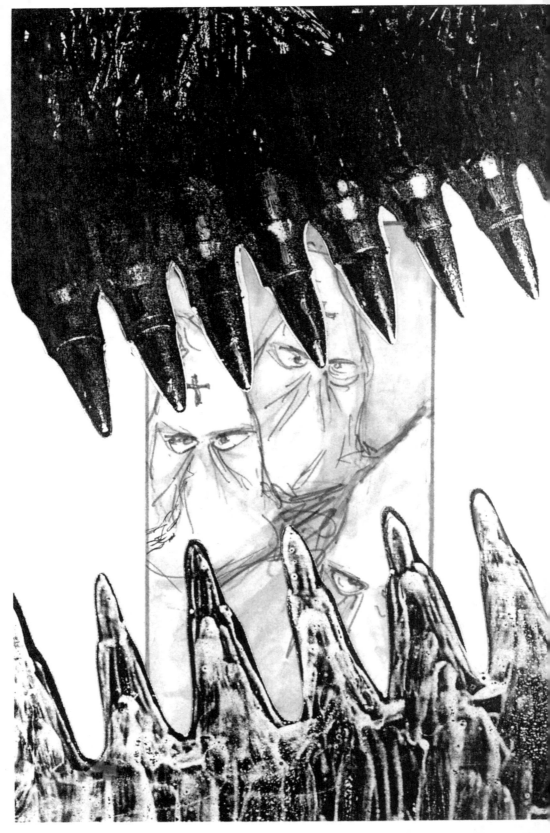

The same evening, a spokesperson for the NOI in Chicago released a statement saying that Malcolm did not speak for, nor in the interests of, the Black Muslim community, and that his sentiments were not shared by the Honorable Elijah Muhammad or any of his followers.

Malcolm was called to Chicago to meet with Elijah Muhammad. Malcolm admitted he made an error in speaking out at a time when the nation was in shock and pain for the loss of a very popular president, but it was too late. The forces in opposition to him had hit the ground running and had closed ranks.

*E*lijah Muhammad told him he would be separated from his duties for 90 days. Always obedient and loyal to his mentor, Malcolm respectfully submitted to censure.

He could not know how deep the conspiracy was to discredit him. On his return to new York he learned the news of his removal had preceded him. He took it as an ominous sign but there was nothing he could do about it.

123

Then Malcolm learned that Elijah Muhammad was guilty of breaking his own strict rules of moral conduct. Three former secretaries had filed paternity suits against the "Gentle Messenger."

MINGHAM BOMB KILL

EGRO GIRLS IN CHURC

OTS FLARE; 2 BOYS SLA

126

While Malcolm was prevented from speaking out, acts of violence against Blacks continued.

He regretted not being able to speak out about the firebombing of the church in Birmingham, Alabama, where six Black children were killed. Instead, Malcolm was concerned with trying to find ways to help Elijah Muhammad save his image. However, after much soul-searching he made a decision to leave the Muslims.

He would continue to speak out and lead the Black community through his own activist organization.

Malcolm X visited his friend Ossie Davis, the noted Black actor, one evening and appeared drained and defeated. The Nation of Islam had been his home. He felt deceived and conned by Elijah Muhammad. Shortly after he announced his separation from the NOI he took a trip to Mecca to establish ties with the world Islamic organization.

Immediately following his announcement in March 1964 of the establishment of two new organizations, Muslim Mosques, Inc. and the Organization of Afro-American Unity, Malcolm set out on a trip to Africa. He called on a highly respected Egyptian diplomat he had met. Mahmoud Shawarbi was a Muslim scholar who introduced Malcolm to the true Islamic faith.

Malcolm's return
to Africa was an
enlightening
experience.

Not only did he get in touch with his ancestral roots, he also made contacts with scholars on the continent who told him the true story of Islam and the truth about America's part in one of the most despicable institutions ever visited on one race by another, slavery based on racism.

For generations hundreds of thousands of men, women and children were torn from their homes, separated from their heritage, and bartered into slavery. After being beaten into submission, they were conditioned for a life of servitude, then crowded into freight cargo ships and delivered to the Americas.

Only the strongest and fittest survived the months-long journey. Only the hardiest and most adaptable withstood the beatings, rapes and torture to out live the horrors of slavery.

Malcolm took the "Hajj," to Mecca where he touched the Holy Kaaba, the Black stone that Allah gave to Muhammad. The Kaaba is the center of the Islamic faith. He visited the great pyramids, and also traveled to Europe and the Middle East.

Everywhere he went people made a fuss over him because he was Malcolm X, the angry Black militant and American Muslim. Malcolm spoke to students in Ghana and nearly caused riots. He was surprised to learn Africans were as incensed as American Blacks over the injustices of racism.

Malcolm visited Lebanon and Algeria and witnessed the suffering of people who were prepared to die to win their liberation from an oppressive government.

He met high-ranking Israeli officials who were also Muslims and some who were enemies of Islam. He realized how deep religious differences ran in the Middle East.

His hosts treated him like royalty. Everywhere he went crowds gathered to touch him and take pictures with him. He was given a new name, conferred on all Muslims who took the Hajj to Mecca, El Hajj Malik Shabazz.

"ARMED WITH THE KNOWLEDGE OF OUR PAST WE CAN CHARTER A COURSE FOR OUR FUTURE. ONLY BY KNOWING WHERE WE'VE BEEN CAN WE KNOW WHERE WE ARE AND LOOK TO WHERE WE WANT TO GO."

Malcolm learned that Africans considered American Blacks long-lost cousins who were welcomed to "come home" to Africa any time they wanted. Marcus Garvey tried and he was jailed and deported. The Black Muslims desired separation and they were discredited as racists and militants.

Malcolm got the idea to charge America with violating the human rights of Afro-Americans.

At a meeting of foreign dignitaries in Africa, Malcolm met Chinese delegates who expressed admiration for his revolutionary ideals.

Malcolm realized the problems of race relations in America as an aberration. He no longer believed that all whites were evil and bigoted. He felt that America's problems were peculiar to America and should be dealt with in that context. However, Malcolm's homecoming was to be a rude awakening. The long, hot summer of 1964 had begun. Rioting and tensions over the war in Vietnam, incidences of police brutality, and civil disobedience had turned America into a war zone.

The minute Malcolm stepped off the plane reporters wanted to know his views. Did he still think all whites were devils? What were his connections to the Blood Brothers, a group of urban Blacks who believed in arming themselves for self-defense?

The Watts riots were touched off when Los Angeles police "invaded" a Black neighborhood and attacked, beat and killed innocent Blacks.

*O*ne by one Malcolm calmly answered each of the questions. The Blood Brothers were a rifle club who kept guns for hunting. Didn't the constitution give all Americans the right to carry arms? He did not believe all whites were devils, only those who behaved like devils. He had nothing to do with the Black Panther Party's policies but he believed in self-defense against the vicious attacks of police or anyone else who invaded our neighborhoods.

Meanwhile the killing and lynching of Blacks continued.

At the beginning of 1964, Black people were told we would have our civil rights broadened. It was in 1964 that the two white civil rights workers were murdered. They were murdered because they were working for voter registration and our civil rights. This was their crime; this was the reason they were murdered. Why should we as a people respect and love anyone who doesn't love or respect us? These were the questions Malcolm and other Black militants raised and directed at America.

WE BELIEVE IN SELF-DEFENSE BY ANY MEANS NECESSARY.

Malcolm applauded the bravery of Vietnamese women who fought and died alongside men in the struggle for liberation from Western oppression.

Malcolm knew he was under surveillance by the government. His home phone was tapped and he knew his every move was being watched, sometimes with no attempt to conceal the fact.

On a visit to Europe, the French government refused to let him enter the country. Malcolm knew the U.S. government had warned them he was going to be assassinated and the French were afraid he would be killed in their country.

Malcolm continued to support the Muslim women who accused Elijah Muhammad of fathering their children, even though Black Muslims who considered him a traitor issued death threats.

Malcolm appeared unbothered by these perils to his safety. He kept his schedule of speaking engagements, refusing to cancel any of them. He regarded it a duty to lend his voice in support of his people in the fight for civil rights no matter where or when.

Malcolm changed his views on interracial relations. He said, "At one time I believed intermarriage between Black and white was forbidden but now I realize that what's important is how two people feel about one another. If two people love one another then that's what's important; it's between the two of them."

The most remarkable thing about Malcolm was his unselfishness. Even while he was under pressure in his personal and public life he still found time to support others in need.

For example, when Harlem Congressman Adam Clayton Powell was being sued, Malcolm was present at every hearing and then at every court appearance to lend his support to the beleaguered minister and representative.

Late in 1964 Malcolm finally met Dr. Martin Luther King, Jr. The two men shook hands and posed for photographers. Malcolm wanted to show he had no ill feelings toward his comrade in the struggle.

What's important is that we both believe in the same things: equality, peace and justice for our people.

"Our methods differ but we are both in the same battle."

Malcolm believed that the destiny of Blacks in America was up to Blacks. We could not, should not, expect any politician, any group, no matter how well meaning, to attain for us what we want. We need to take our destiny in our hands, do whatever we must to obtain our freedom, our human and civil rights.

Malcolm pressed on as a loner and he seemed fragile and vulnerable. His fledging organizations, the O.A.A.U. and Muslim Mosques, Inc., were not doing well. He told Mike Wallace in a television interview, "we have few members and no money."

Malcolm had never managed his own organization outside of the Black Muslims. He had always been a loyal soldier. But he was still the voice of a vast majority in the ghettos of America. He had always spoken for the Black community. He always would.

In the last months of 1964, Malcolm left for Saudi Arabia and parts east to raise funds to construct a new headquarters for his Muslim Mosque, Inc. and the Organization of Afro-American Unity. This time the U.S. government was watching him closely.

He visited Switzerland, England, Africa, Kuwait and the Netherlands. The State Department had been trailing his movements and kept a close watch on his activities on his final trip overseas. His fund-raising did not go well because many countries were still heavily dependent on U.S. foreign aid and did not want to put their relationship at risk.

Malcolm was lobbying to take the race problem of the United States before the Charter of Human Rights of the United Nations. He felt the injustices of bigotry, racism and prejudice were comparable to war crimes and should be presented in the same way that the Nuremberg Trials brought the criminals of World War II before the World Court.

He wanted his Organization of Afro-American Unity to shake the world.

*H*is attempts to get support for his plan to bring the United States before the World Court for human rights violations was also unsuccessful. Malcolm returned to the United States disappointed but undaunted. He continued to remind Afro-Americans (having vowed never to use the term negroes again), that Lincoln did not free the slaves because slavery is a state of mind.

Under siege from all sides, Malcolm appeared exhausted near the end.

Malcolm was now a national figure. Suddenly the police were at his disposal, not to harass him but to protect him. Malcolm refused their protection. He did not want to give the appearance of being afraid for his life.

In the days leading up to February 1965, Malcolm stepped up his activities as though his time was running out.

He said that he had no respect for any man who didn't wear a watch. Time was one of the most important factors in a man's life. In early January a cryptic message in <u>Muhammad Speaks</u> hinted that the voices of all traitors to the nation would soon be silenced. Malcolm told some close aids, "It wouldn't be long now. The end is near."

BERNARD
AQUINA
DOCTOR 91 ©

Malcolm modified his views about a woman's place in the struggle since leaving the Black Muslims. He felt that Black women had a very important role in keeping the Black family together.

He fought hard to keep the Black community together and frowned on groups that tried to recruit Black women away from this primary responsibility, such as the Feminist Liberation Organization and NOW.

On the 19th of February his home in Queens, New York, was firebombed. He had been ordered to vacate the house, which was owned by the Nation of Islam, after losing a court battle to remain.

One of Malcolm's
last messages to the community was to
look out for the children. They are the last
hope of America. It's too late
for grownups.

Malcolm kept his speaking engagements, even on the day of the firebombing.
Back in New York on the 21st of February,
1965, Malcolm was scheduled to address
a meeting of his O.A..A.U.
He phoned his wife Betty and told her he
wanted her and the girls to attend a
meeting at the Audobon Ballroom. He had
a feeling it would be the last time he saw
his family.

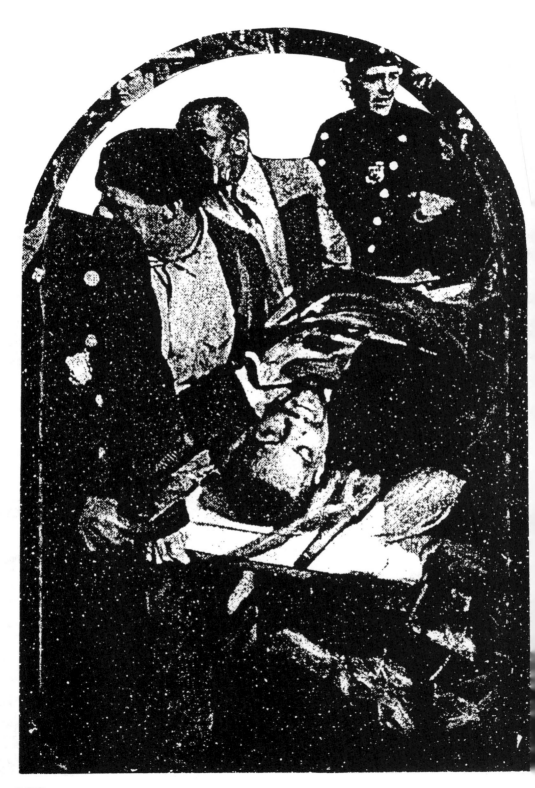

Like the premonition his mother had the night his father was killed, Malcolm was once again about to relive a tragedy, his last in life. El-Hajj, Malik, Shabazz, Omowali, Malcolm "X," Detroit Red. Malcolm Little, seventh son of Earl and Louise Little, was gunned down as he was about to address the small gathering. The last words he uttered were, "It's O.K. brothers, settle down." The three men in the front section who had created the commotion suddenly whirled on Malcolm with guns drawn and shot him in the chest. His friend, Ossie Davis, eulogized Malcolm at his funeral: "We have lost our shinning Black Prince."

Malcolm, our shinning Black Prince, was dead before the ambulance left the scene.

BIBLIOGRAPHY AND SOURCES

Malcolm X, The Man and His Times
Edited by John Henrik Clark, Earl Grant
and Betty Shabazz, 1969
Collier-Macmillian, Toronto, Canada, 1969

The Autobiography of Malcolm X
Alex Haley, 1964
Ballantine Books & Grove Press, 1973-1990

Malcolm X Speaks
Selected Speeches and Statements
with notes by George Breitman
Grove Press, New York, 1965

The Last Year of Malcolm X,
The Evolution of a Revolutionary
George Breitman
Schocken Books, New York, 1968

Harlem: The Making of a Ghetto
Gilbert Osofsky
Harper-Torch Books, New York, 1968

The Oratory of Negro Leaders: 1900-1968
Marcus Hanna Boulware, 1969
Negro Universities Press, Westport, Connecticut

A televised broadcast of, "Like It Is"
Host and Narrator Gil Noble
First aired February 22, 1975

Ebony and Jet Magazine
The Donnell Library

Time-Life Magazine
The Broadcast, Moving Images and
Sound Recording Center
of the Schomburg Library,
Harlem, New York

Who Was Marcus Garvey
Sayyid Al Imaam
Isa Al Haadi Al Mahdi, 1988

All Our Kin
Strategies for Survival in a Black Community
Carol B. Stack, 1974
Harper and Row

Visuals, photographs and previously unpublished artwork of
Aquina Productions, Visual Communications, NYC.

Where Do We Go from Here: Chaos or Community?
Martin Luther King, Jr., 1967
Beacon Press

Paul Robeson Tributes and Selected Writings
Compiled from the Paul Robeson Archives, 1976
Robeson Archives, New York, NY